A FRIEND

SHOULD BE

RADICAL,

FANATICAL,

BUT

MOST OF ALL

MATHEMATICAL

A FRIEND SHOULD BE
RADICAL, FANATICAL,
BUT MOST OF All
MATHEMATICAL

BILLY SPRAGUE

ILLUSTRATIONS BY DENNAS DAVIS

WOLGEMUTH & HYATT, PUBLISHERS, INC.
BRENTWOOD, TENNESSEE

Wolgemuth & Hyatt, Publishers, Inc.
1749 Mallory Lane, Suite 110
Brentwood, Tennessee 37027

To
Jim Weber,
My Mathematical
Friend

A FRIEND SHOULD BE RADICAL

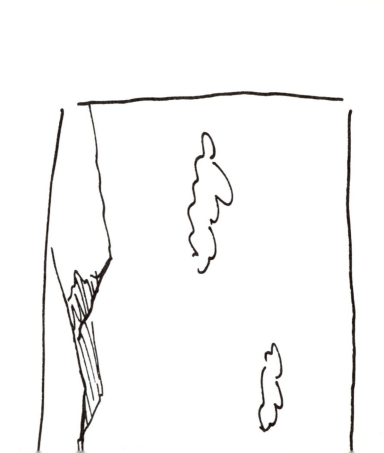

HE
SHOULD LOVE
WHEN YOU'RE
UNLOVABLE

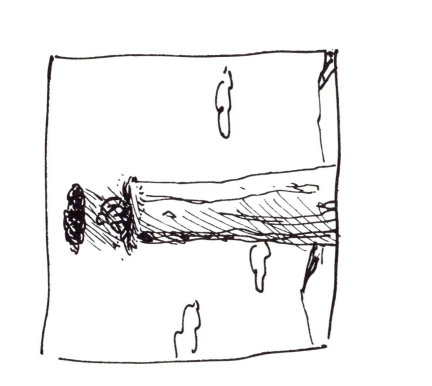

HUG
WHEN YOU'RE
UNHUGGABLE

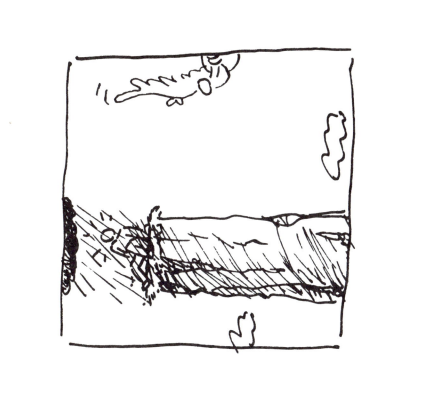

AND
BEAR WHEN
YOU'RE
UNBEARABLE

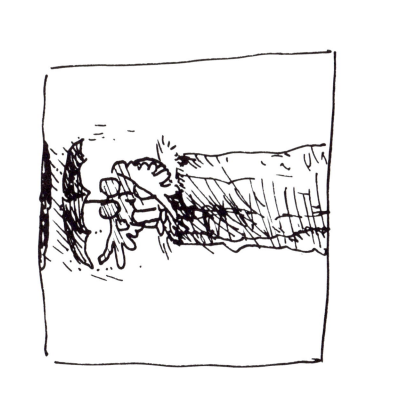

A FRIEND
SHOULD BE

FANATICAL

HE SHOULD
CHEER
WHEN THE WHOLE
WORLD
BOOS

DANCE
WHEN YOU
GET
GOOD NEWS

AND CRY
WHEN
YOU CRY
too

BUT MOST OF ALL ...

A FRIEND
SHOULD
BE
MATHEMATICAL

HE SHOULD
MULTIPLY
THE
JOY

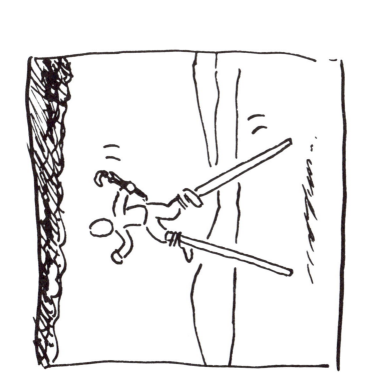

DIVIDE
THE
SORROW

SUBTRAKT
THE
PAST

AND ADD
TO
TOMORROW

HE SHOULD
CALCULATE THE
NEED, DEEP
IN YOUR
HEART

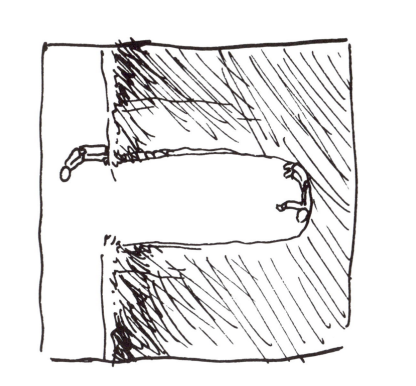

BIGGER
BE
AND

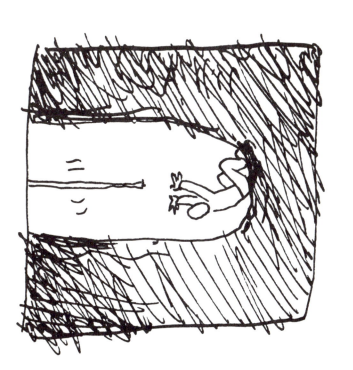

THAN THE
SUM
OF ALL
HIS PARTS

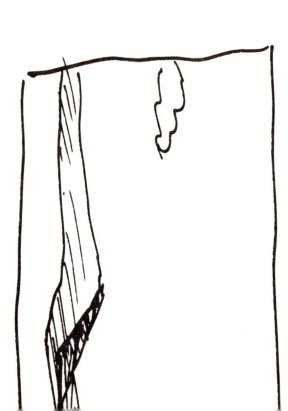

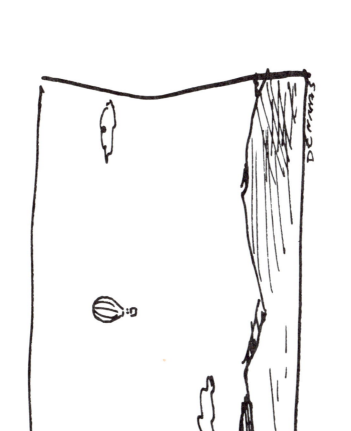